# Walking in the World as a Friend

## ESSENTIAL QUAKER PRACTICES

*Nadine Clare Hoover*

*Live up to the light thou hast, and more will be granted thee.*
*~ Caroline Fox, 1840*

Hoover, Nadine Clare
    *Walking in this World as a Friend: Essential Quaker Practice*
ISBN  978-0-9828492-7-9

1. Quakers HRCC97
2. Interfaith HRAF
3. Mysticism HRLK2
4. Religion and Beliefs HR

# *Table of Contents*

### *Part III: RELIGIOUS SOCIETY*

# Acknowledgements

I am grateful to the Quaker religious educators from around the world who gather in North America with the Quaker Religious Education Collaborative. Our practical and pragmatic nature helps keep the simplicity and complexity of Quaker practice fresh and alive with the Spirit. The QREC Steering Committee brings a fresh openness, honesty, and spiritual hospitality that comes with genuine practice.

Specifically Beth Collea, Sita Diehl, Marty Grundy, and Liz Yeats reached out, encouraged, read, commented, and kept this work on track. The support of the Thomas H. & Mary Williams Shoemaker Fund made this work possible, particularly during the pandemic. I hope it lives up to their mission to renew and strengthen the Religious Society of Friends.

I am also grateful to the Acehnese on the north tip of Sumatra. They live harsh lives, having grown up in a thirty-year, heavily U.S. funded war. Still, they welcomed me, taught me, and engaged in mutual discernment. The crucible of their struggle, tempered the clarity reflected here.

The Alfred Monthly Meeting over the last half of the twentieth century, Tallahassee Monthly Meeting from 1986-1999, and Gay Howard allowed me to experience Quaker practice, the joy of Quaker community, and the daily miracles of opening our lives to the guidance of the Living Spirit. Having experienced communities that focus on the simple core practices, I understand why Quakers often moved as whole communities. Mutual discernment grows and matures over time in inexplicable ways.

Thank you to everyone who stops, softens, listens, and yields, with courage, enthusiasm, humility, and conviction. "May the long time sun shine upon us, all love surround us, and the pure light within us, guide our way on" (Mike Heron, 1967).

~

*Dearly beloved Friends,*
*these things we do not lay upon you as a*
*rule or form to walk by, but that all,*
*with the measure of light which is pure and holy,*
*may be guided; & so in the light walking and abiding,*
*these may be fulfilled in the Spirit, not from the letter,*
*for the letter killeth, but the Spirit giveth life.*

*~ Balby Elders, 1656*

~

# *Foreword*

We were at the 2019 Quaker Religious Education Collaborative (QREC) conference. Right at the end of the plenary session on "Claiming the Living Roots of Our Faith," someone asked, "What does a Quaker do that makes us a Quaker?"

The general response was, "We do our own thing; we find our own way." Since Quakers have no dogma or creed and we respect each person, we tend to speak for ourselves, not for others. But this can fuel individualism. Quaker practice is communal. Individualism erodes community and thus undermines Quaker practice.

So, over lunch I wrote a few approaches to teaching Quaker practice for either youth or adults on flip chart papers. Then QREC asked me to produce those as materials for Friends Meetings. Beth Collea, Liz Yeats, Sita Diehl, and Marty Grundy offered invaluable input and feedback. We organized them into four areas:

- **Three Key Quaker Roles:** Minister, Steward, and Witness. Quakers commit to three key roles as a minister, steward, and witness. Quakers laid down the laity and recognized each person as a minister, a Child of God, with direct access to the Divine. We took on the roles of minister—nurturing our inward lives, steward—shaping our outward lives, and witness—expressing faith and practice in our public lives.

- **Experiences of the Spirit: Convincement and Conviction**. Quakers experience the Living Spirit that speaks to our human condition. We experience the power and grace of the Spirit in easy and hard times, in every person, every moment, everywhere. We celebrate the beauty and value of life for the pure joy of it.

- **Experiment with the Spirit: Conversion of Manners.** Quakers experiment with allowing the Spirit to shape and guide our daily lives through our human faculties of love, conscience and discernment. The Spirit affirms the good and loving, and illuminates the broken and unloving, within ourselves, others, and our institutions.

- **Religious Society of Friends: Essential Quaker Structures**. Quaker practice is a mystical ecology of practice, not fanatical, *laissez-faire*, or blind faith. In our practice, Spirit transforms individuals tempered and tested by the community, who temper and test other communities. This reveals societal guidance that shapes the lives of individuals, creating a regenerative ecology of practice.

In recent generations, Quakers identified group agreements to practice, which you may introduce at any session or in the meeting as a whole, that help create a beloved community together.

### *Agreements to Practice*

- Affirm myself and others, no put downs or put ups.
- Stop, listen, don't interrupt.
- Speak simply and honestly without fear of mistakes.
- Speak from my experience, not other's without permission.
- Tend emotions, then speak directly to someone if in dispute.
- Ask for and offer hospitality, feedback and help.
- Make friends not enemies with people who are similar and different.
- Use what I need and share the rest fairly.
- Use my rights to pass and to consultation.
- Volunteer myself only, not others.
- Care for each person, the community and the natural world.
- Live in integrity with life's transforming power.

*Expanded from the Alternatives to Violence Project • AVP.International*

# How to Use This Book

This series offers rich descriptions of experiential ways to embody Quaker practice with activities for First Day School classes, meeting events, or study groups. It worked for Fox and Fell, Mott and Woolman, and so many others; it can work for us, too. To work, we must lower our defenses and listen with our child's mind, curious to see what will happen. We must engage in the practices anew and expect fresh inspiration.

This series may be useful in bits and pieces or as an entire sequence for Quaker religious education for youth or adults. Working both within and across age cohorts keeps Quaker practice vibrant. This does not need an expert. Any group may read the booklet, listen to the videos, do the activities, and learn together. Spiritual life and practice grow as we pay attention to them. But it does benefit from participants who experience the Spirit, yield to spiritual guidance in daily life, and are vulnerable and authentic in sharing their Quaker faith and practice.

You may read from this text or view an accompanying video as an introduction to an activity. You may feel awkward, inadequate, or overwhelmed by the instructions at first. But the longer you stick with them and practice them as instructed, the more natural they become.

Materials you might like to have include: this text, video access, personal journals, and activity instructions to hand out or post. The Core Self Drawing activity requires paper and oil pastels or crayons, but the more vibrant the color, the better.

The accompanying video series may be found on the Quaker Religious Education Collaborative website. View them on their own or as an introduction to an activity:

**Key Quaker Roles (total 22:09)**
Key Quaker Roles: Minister, Steward, Witness (3:31)
Being a Minister (6:8)
Being a Steward (6:7)
Being a Witness (5:37)
Being a Companion (4:17)

**Experience and the Experiment (total 21:11)**
Spiritual Convincement (5:8)
Spiritual Conviction (7:43)
The Experiment with the Living Spirit (8:20)

**Essential Quaker Structures (total 56:54)**
Ecology of Practice: Essential Quaker Structures (8:32)
Quaker Worship (6:50)
Spiritual Companions (7:53) and Questions (2:31)
Monthly Meeting (9:55)
Meetings of Ministers, Stewards, or Witnesses (6:20)
Yearly Meeting Faith and Practice (5:40)
Bearing Witness to the Living Spirit (9:13)

You may enjoy watching a video and discussing it. But talking about something is very different from experiencing it. So I recommend watching a video, taking the time needed to practice, then reflecting on the experience of the practice. We learn from experience and reflection, and then sharing our insights with others. Without the Spirit of the doing of it, one will never know it. But we must also find the language to talk about it, invite others in, and pass on to future generations. The final test of discernment is the fruit it bears. The final measure of this booklet is the joy it brings in creating loving, conscientious communities and society.

# Preface: Background on Quaker Practice

Quaker practice grew out of a movement known as The Seekers, who sat in silence turning to God, waiting and expecting revelation and guidance. The first structure of Quakers was continuing this form of Meeting for Worship, waiting and expecting messages for themselves as individuals and as a people. Today, Friends may enjoy other forms of worship and celebration, but continue this practice of seeking direct divine guidance and yielding to it.

The second structure was the Spiritual Companions. Early Friends gave each other attention, tended to healing, and exchanged feedback to grow in our spiritual lives. Companions were both committed to the spiritual experiment with their lives. They bolstered and tempered each other's ministry. In this way, Quaker ministry grew.

As Quakers followed an Inward Guide, they needed to discern inspiration from egos or distress. Other sects turned to religious hierarchy for control. But a formative, uniquely Quaker insight was the role of community to test and record discernment. In their experience, the eternal was universal.

So the third structure was the local Monthly Meeting where individuals testified to revelation guiding their faith and practice. The meeting tested their discernment by whether Friends sensed the life and power of the Spirit in their testimony. If so, they recorded it with the name in the meeting minutes. If it were true for everyone, they recorded a corporate testimony and shared it with other meetings.

Sandra Cronk pointed out that we should not embark on Quaker practice lightly. If you turn to the Inward Guide, you must yield. To refuse to yield plants dis-ease. The experience of Inward Guidance may feel either petty or overwhelming because truth does not usually come packaged to our size. Quaker practice is to yield and allow truth to change us, regardless of whether it fits well or suits us.

Contemporary individualism has a significant erosive effect on Quaker practice, because Quaker practice is communal. Individualism diminishes the vibrancy of Quaker communities.

Beth Collea describes, *"The hesitation to deeply share within one's meeting is often encoded in our culture as Friends, another manifestation of individualism. It is revitalizing for a meeting to have Friends step gently over this limiting threshold. We can think of this as 'truing up the meeting' and bringing it back to some of its primary work (of love and communion)!"* From Lessons from Thriving Meetings, QREC (quakers4re.org)

In addition, many factors disrupt and obstruct Quaker practice:

- Population increase and mobility disrupt the community.
- Speed disrupts the ability to stop, listen, digest, and discern.
- Toxicity of industrial life, food, and water exhausts us.
- Sleep deprivation intoxicates and numbs us.
- Computerization proliferates indirect relationships, which obscure sources of ecological and social ills, and their potential remedies.

These factors weaken Quaker practice and diminish the vigor in our work and witness in the world. Quakers no longer lead in exposing exploitation, environmental devastation, or oppressive cycles of prejudice and privilege. Others no longer turn to Quakers for societal guidance on how to form beloved communities or societies, especially on issues of securing safe haven, governance, healthcare, education, justice, and peace.

Doing what's true and loving in every relationship and every moment in the face of the challenges may lead to prosperity or suffering. Regardless of the outcome, doing so liberates and satisfies the soul. We can look our persecutor in the eye with compassion. George Fox's letter to ministers from prison in Cornwall conveys this bold nature of Quaker practice. We recommend reading, even posting, the full text of George Fox's famous letter to ministers in 1656, which may continue to challenge us today.

## Overview of Quaker Practice

| I have experienced the Living Spirit… | …that speaks to my condition. | I choose to yield to let it shape and guide my life, … | …test discernment and record testimony, faith, practice, queries, and advices in community. |
|---|---|---|---|
| *loving,* | *healing,* | *seeking,* | *finding, …* |
| CONVINCEMENT | CONVICTION | EXPERIMENT | PUBLISHING OF LOVE & TRUTH |
| MINISTER | STEWARD | WITNESS | |
| *Tending the inward life.* | | *Tending the outward forms.* | |
| Listening | Lamentation | Journaling | Scripture Study |
| Solitude | Healing & Grounding | Experiment in Daily Life | Monthly Meeting (for feedback) |
| Worship | Spiritual Companions | Tests of Discernment | Liberty of Conscience |
| Celebration | Counsel and Care | Available & Prepared | Recording: Minutes, Faith & Practice, Testimony, Advices & Queries, |

*Friends,*

*In the power of life and wisdom, and dread of the Lord God of life, and heaven, and earth, dwell; that in the wisdom of God over all ye may be preserved, and be a terror to all the adversaries of God, and a dread, answering that of God in them all, spreading the Truth abroad, awakening the witness, confounding deceit, gathering up out of transgression into the life, the covenant of light and peace with God.*

*Let all nations hear the word by sound or writing. Spare no place, spare not tongue nor pen, but be obedient to the Lord God and go through the world and be valiant for the Truth upon earth; tread and trample all that is contrary under.*

*Keep in the wisdom of God that spreads over all the earth, the wisdom of the creation, that is pure. Live in it; that is the word of the Lord God to you all, do not abuse it; and keep down and low; and take heed of false joys that will change.*

*Bring all into the worship of God. Plough up the fallow ground... And none are ploughed up but he who comes to the principle of God in him which he hath transgressed. Then he doth service to God; then the planting and the watering and the increase from God cometh. So the ministers of the Spirit must minister to the Spirit that is transgressed and in prison, which hath been in captivity in every one; whereby with the same Spirit people must be led out of captivity up to God, the Father of spirits, and do service to him and have unity with him, with the Scriptures and with one another. And this is the word of the Lord God to you all, and a charge to you all in the presence of the living God: be patterns, be examples in all countries, places, islands, nations, wherever you come, that your carriage and life may preach among all sorts of people, and to them; then you will come to walk cheerfully over the world, answering that of God in every one.*

*~ George Fox, 1656*
*Britain Yearly Meeting Faith and Practice 19.32*

*Part I*

~

# THREE KEY QUAKER ROLES

~

*"It is true that in a Friends meeting the responsibility for worship and ministry rests upon each and every member; but it is also true that Friends, like others, must somewhat rely for their awakening upon those who are more in God's spirit and power than the average."*

~ N. Jean Toomer, 1894-1967

~

# Chapter 1

~

# Minister, Steward, and Witness

One approach that can help us embody Quaker practice is to consider how to carry out the three key roles we take on as Quakers: minister, steward, and witness. Quaker practice is communal. Paying attention to these key roles weaves our internal work into our relationships in the community. Quakers laid down the laity, not the ministry; we are each ministers. We each take responsibility for the spiritual work of the Religious Society of Friends.

A Friend once blurted out, "But Meeting shouldn't take over my entire life!" Then I saw the realization across her face as she said, "Oh," acknowledging that that was exactly the intent. We give over our entire lives to the Spirit. We become a pattern that bears witness to God manifest in every relationship of life: changing, transforming, empowering us and our beloved community. It's not something we dabble in, it's a whole-body experience, a life-changing commitment.

As Quakers, we experience the Spirit in the direct relationships among people and with nature in the fabric of life. Our spiritual lives grow in relationship with others and the natural world. The meeting is more than the people attending on a particular day. Every member has a unique experience of the Spirit. So we each play a unique part in forming who "we" are as a community and may be the source of the insight another needs. The quality of our growth in our primary roles grows in relationship to others and determines the quality and maturity of the body of the Meeting.

As a minister, we tend our inward lives. As a steward, we tend our outward lives to reflect the inward life. And as a witness, we tend our public lives to reflect the Spirit in society. Quakers open, listen, and seek. We testify to what we find. Quakers are each personally seekers, finders, and healers. Some are healers by nature, but each of us needs to heal in order to become whole and well. These are personal responsibilities, not community roles.

People are recognized as elders when others turn to them for guidance and counsel  because of the depth of their practice and attention to others. Some people are recognized as public Friends when others see their lives and speech reflect Quaker faith and practice with humility and courage. Some people are recognized as clerks when others turn to them to articulate the authentic sense of the meeting in matters of concern, because of their ability to listen for and capture the sense of the meeting in words. Being an elder, public Friend, or clerk is not an identity one takes on such as being a minister, steward, or witness. And such positions should not be used to have power over the meeting, but rather power to draw the meeting into the life of the Spirit and record and reflect our testimony in the world.

Quakerism is not an idea or notion we imagine being true. It's a practice in ourselves and in a community that humbles and changes us, which takes time, patience, consistency, and openness, even in the face of challenges. Our roles as a minister, steward, and witness change, temper, humble, and liberate us.

## Being a Minister

As ministers, we tend to our inward lives. We tend the inward life in oneself, others, and the community both in the easy, glorious, all-is-well times and in the hard, broken times of inadequacy and failure.

Ministers invest in our own spiritual lives and experience through the gifts of solitude, stillness, and contemplative prayer. We carry this into our everyday lives. We open to the Spirit, seek revelation, celebrate life, offer gratitude, heal to become whole, and reintegrate the broken parts of us as people and as a community.

As ministers, we experience our daily lives as praying without ceasing. We study religious texts and learn the language of the inner landscape, in Bill Taber's words. Quakers engage in the tendering and tempering of spiritual companions to grow in our spiritual understanding and expression. We arrive at meetings for worship fresh and prepared, genuinely seeking guidance, expecting spiritual revelation, and offering vocal ministry.

Then we offer spiritual support, feedback, hospitality, counsel, and testimony to others. We allow others to see our example in the richness of our full humanity. Ministers model and encourage spiritual life and companionship within the meeting community.

## Being a Steward

As stewards, we tend to our outward lives. Quakers shape our outward lives to reflect the inward experience. We live faithfully. As ministers we trust direct, mystical experience of the Divine. As stewards we seek integrity by yielding to spiritual guidance. Stewards care for the outward lives, livelihoods, and temporal needs of ourselves, our families, community, society, and the natural world in which we live. We reflect the inward experience in outward form, putting our lives in order to be prepared and available, if called.

We submit every aspect of our lives to spiritual scrutiny. Humans can discern. Discernment is the ability to comprehend the inner nature and relationship of things, especially when obscure, that leads to keen insight and judgment. To develop, we must test our discernment. The primary tests are: a sense of the Spirit; persistence in silence; simplicity; a sense of being either trivial or impossible and not willful or desired; integrity in honesty, authenticity, and consistency; documentation in texts of other spiritual communities; writing or expression; reflection and feedback from others; and fruit of the Spirit: love, joy, peace, patience, kindness, generosity, faithfulness, gentleness, and self-control (Gal. 5:22-23).

Note, the word *steward* replaces the historic term, *overseer*. In biblical times, overseers managed the outward forms such as ritual objects and collected alms for the poor. The term later became used for those controlling enslaved peoples, so we prefer the term *steward*.

## Being a Witness

As witnesses, we tend to our public lives. Witness for Quakers takes several forms. We:

- Let our lives speak through the fruits of faithful living. We become examples of God manifest in human form that witness to the fruits of the Spirit: love, joy, peace, strength, compassion, beauty, truth, equality, and liberty.
- Testify in our meeting community to the insight and directions of our spiritual experiment. We season our testimony with spiritual companions, before asking the monthly meeting for reflection and feedback. This opens our experiment with spiritual life and guidance to others.
- Are called on to assess if something is loving, true, right, and just, because others have seen the results of our discernment and find us reliable, insightful witnesses.
- Testify in the larger community and society to the Spirit in human affairs, to what is loving, true, and just that is essential for a religious society. Quaker practice is not an individual practice of individual enlightenment, but of forming a beloved community and society.
- Document in public record how the Spirit is manifest in a religious society over generations. We seek a beloved society in which we order every relationship with others and the natural world in accord with the Spirit. So we enter our insights and practices into public record, through writing, art, song, curriculum, law, and court record.

Both the unearned sufferings and developmental advantages of Quaker practice carry obligations and opportunities to witness to the Spirit in our communities and larger society.

# Chapter 2

~

# *Activities to Explore Quaker Roles*

This chapter describes how to host a Worship Sharing, Spiritual Companion Group, or Friendly Faith and Practice Study to explore the three key Quaker roles individually or as a group.

## *Worship Sharing*

Worship Sharing is a time to listen to others and describe your own experiences of the Spirit, how you have changed, and your spiritual direction. This format develops experiences and skills that enrich vocal ministry in Meeting for Worship and discernment in Monthly Meeting.

Let your guard down and experience life wholly, beyond fear, and live into your sense of the movement of the Spirit within, describing the nuances. Describe how you sense Spirit within something or not. Notice the obstacles or hurdles, inner strengths to overcome them, and liberty and joy that comes with living in accord with love and conscience. Develop a language of the inner landscape and how you reflect that inward experience in outward form.

Read these instructions out loud at the start of each worship sharing, even with experienced participants. Post or hand out instruction cards:

### *Worship Sharing*

Settle into silence.

Read a topic, verse, or query.

Ask if it is clear; clarify as needed.

Give everyone a chance to speak, before speaking again.

Speak from your own experience.

Leave silence between speakers.

Be open, teachable, and changed by what you hear.

Select a topic or query to announce before the meeting. If worship sharing is new to the group, choose a general question such as, "How do I experience the Living Spirit?" or "How do I live my daily life as a Friend?" If the group has more experience with Worship Sharing, pick a topic or query that is salient for the meeting at this time.

To explore growing as a minister, steward, and witness, hold one session on all three roles, or three sessions, one on each role. Queries for one Worship Sharing session on all three roles:

- How are you growing as a minister, steward, and witness?
- How do you tend the inward life, reflect the inward life in your outward life, and express the inward life in your public life?
- How do you share through vocal ministry, testimony, and public record?

Queries for three Worship Sharing sessions to reflect on what each of the roles means to us:

### Minister

- How am I growing as a minister to tend the inward life in myself and others?
- How do I share revelation through vocal ministry?

### Steward

- How am I growing as a steward to reflect my inward experience of the Spirit in the outward forms of my life and community?
- How do I share guidance through testimony in my monthly meeting?

**Witness**

- How am I growing as a witness to articulate in our Faith and Practice or through public testimony or public record our insights and practices?

Queries for three Worship Sharing sessions to focus on the central work of each of the three roles:

- *Continuing Revelation.* Ask, What is God revealing through me, for me? ...for us as a people? ...for the wider society? Do I keep a spiritual journal? Do I bring my testimony to my spiritual companions and monthly meeting? Do I share, test, record, and publish continuing revelation as revealed to me? Schedule this worship sharing every 4-6 months or annually in the meeting.

- *Daily Living as a Friend.* State the topic as sharing on daily living as a Friend--simple but rich. You may also ask, How are you experimenting with the Spirit in your life? What do you need to have or let go of to stay aware of the Spirit? Are your life and house in order? Are you available and prepared to respond, if called?

- *Bearing Witness.* Ask, How do I testify to the Living Spirit in my private and public life? How am I a terror to the adversaries of God? How do I do justice, love mercy, and walk humbly with my God? How do I think and act out of faith rather than a crisis of faith? Schedule this worship sharing every 4-6 months or annually in the meeting.

## *Spiritual Companion Groups*

Host a single session of Spiritual Companions in triads to consider Quaker roles. Give each person attention for a full 10 minutes on the topic: "How am I growing in my role as minister, steward, and/or witness?"

The focus person may reflect in silence, may discharge emotion, or may share insights. Then give 5 minutes for the listener(s) to reflect back key statements in the speaker's words. Ask the groups to switch focus people on time.

Part of the practice is to balance giving and receiving attention to everyone. Needing excessive attention or giving up attention are both common forms of reenacting trauma or patterns of oppression, so please switch on time. After 45 minutes, return to the whole group. Take three minutes to write implications for your life in your journal. Then take 10 minutes to share in a pair (not one of your earlier companions) what you learned from doing this. Close with 10 minutes in the whole group to share implications for us as a people. This is a simple small group format. Spiritual companions are an essential Quaker structure and described in more detail in that section below.

## *Keep a Log or Journal*

Keep a personal journal to track your experiment with the Spirit in your life. Ask and it will be given to you; seek and you will find; knock and the door will be opened to you. (Matthew 7:7; Luke 11:9) Friends ask, seek, and knock, and we document what is given, what we find, and how the way opens in a journal or log, which we test with companions, and bring seasoned statements of faith and practice to the community. In a journal make notes on:

- Revelation, insights and practices.
- Testimonies affirmed by companions.
- Messages for us as a people.

Experiment with the Spirit in daily life, and keep track of your practices, revelation, and changes:

- *Stop...* in body, mind, tension, distress, and open to the Spirit.
- *Seek...* with companions tend emotions, queries, and insights.
- *Celebrate and be grateful...* celebrate the gift of life given freely.
- *Be changed...* oneself, experiment with allowing the Spirit to guide and shape one's life.
- *Heal...* discharge emotions, reprocess memories, integrate the core self, and take care.
- *Testify...* in community, reflect back what was said, offer feedback whether you can feel the power of the Spirit in it, and

record insights and practices.

• *Bear witness...* apply faith and practice in all life and society and document for other cultures and future generations.

You should expect privacy and not ask or be asked to share one's journal with others. At the same time, you may find that you want to share excerpts or portions of your journal with your companion group or meeting, or even publish portions, but that should be entirely up to you, not at the request of others.

Write palm-of-your-hand journals, by taking 10 minutes to list major experiences, insights, or practices that formed your spiritual life, or formed you as a minister, steward, or witness. Then write 250-500 words on each one. Publish and share them informally in your meeting. Read historic Friends journals and discuss them as a book club.

## *Friendly Faith and Practice Study*

For human beings, learning often overrides intuition. We learn to walk, whereas most animals walk instinctively within a few minutes or hours. Our unique intellect offers many gifts, but also often requires study when we wish it would "just happen."

We use the Friendly Faith and Practice Study queries to study religious texts or a Yearly Meeting Faith and Practice. I adapted the queries slightly from Spears & Spears (1997):

> *Friendly Faith and Practice Study*
> What are the main points in this passage?
> What new light do I find in this particular reading?
> How is this passage true to my experience or our experience?
> What problems do I have with this text?
> What are the implications for my life and for us as a people?

We may use these queries to study our own or any other Yearly Meeting's Faith and Practice as well. I am particularly fond of Britain Yearly Meeting's Faith and Practice. Select a focus text to announce before the meeting. Review the questions, then read the entry aloud. Settle into silence, and speak out of the silence. Ask people to all take responsibility for sharing the time equally. Go around the circle and speak to each query briefly, or go around once and speak to any or all the queries, one person at a time. Estimate the time you have, leaving time (usually 15-20 minutes) for reflection on how it felt to do the practice and any feedback to the facilitator at the end.

Gather copies of your Yearly Meetings' Faith and Practice. Read quotes and advice for ministers, stewards (formerly overseers), and witnesses. Use the Friendly Faith and Practice Study queries to guide the reflection and speaking. Go around the circle for each question, listen to each person, then invite final comments before proceeding to the next question. Debrief on the experience at the end. What did you notice? What did you learn? What did you like or not like? Any suggestions for next time?

Gather copies of many other Yearly Meeting's Faith and Practices. Have each person research the three roles in different Yearly Meetings' Faith and Practices. Note similarities and differences and discover added details and insights. Bring testimony to your Monthly Meeting on critical insights or practices for each role that are missing or need to be removed from the guidance of your own Faith and Practice to your community.

*Part II*

~

# THE SPIRIT
# IN OUR LIVES

~

*I expect to pass through this world but once;*
*any good thing therefore I can do,*
*or any kindness that I can show*
*to any fellow creature, let me do it now;*
*let me not defer or neglect it,*
*for I shall not pass this way again.*

~ Stephen Grellet, Quaker c. 1800

~

## Chapter 3

~

# Experiences of
# the Living Spirit

*Quakers experience the Living Spirit and so we are convinced,
and celebrate the beauty and value of life for the pure joy of it.*

## Convincement

As Quakers, we have met the Spirit; it is irrefutable and convincing. As I would be if I met you. If someone told me you did not exist, it would not matter. I would be convinced, because I had met you and knew you existed. And so when we experience the Living Spirit. Our practice is to notice the vibrancy of the Living Spirit anew in every moment and to live in the joy of being alive. We were called the Children of God. We need to bring our 'child's mind' to delighting in every part of the day from morning through nighttime.

Margaret Fell (1652) describes her moment of convincement, "I cried in my spirit to the Lord, 'We are all thieves, we are all thieves, we have taken the Scriptures in words and know nothing of them in ourselves'.... I saw it was the truth, and I could not deny it; and I did as the apostle saith, I 'received the truth in the love of it'. And it was opened to me so clear that I had never a tittle in my heart against it; but I desired the Lord that I might be kept in it, and then I desired no greater portion."

Quakers experience that essence of life that George Fox (1657) called the eternal, that "which was before the world was." Experiences of the Living Spirit may come as special mountain-top, glorious, or all-is-well moments. They may come as significant moments of insight or grief. But they may come as we delight in the ordinary breeze, sun, stars, blossoms, gentle smiles, or daily wonder at being alive. We may notice our breath and heartbeat and wonder about their source. Life is valuable. I am alive. I am valuable. Nothing I can say or do can make me any more valuable than I am right now. We've arrived. This is life, this is enough. A. Barratt Brown (1932) describes this so well, "It is a bold and colossal claim that we put forward – that the whole of life is sacramental, that there are innumerable 'means of grace' by which God is revealed and communicated – through nature and through human fellowship and through a thousand things that may become the 'outward and visible sign' of 'an inward and spiritual grace.'"

Such an awareness softens and opens us, without possessing. In fact, we call ourselves Friends because we experience this inward tendering. Jesus said I will no longer call you servants, I will call you friends if you do what I direct, and that is to love each other (John 15). Love is to feel a tender affection for and a sense of the preciousness of another, while free to take leave without ill judgment or retribution. Life comes and life goes, that's its nature. Let go, don't hold on, and celebrate life anew each day.

As the Religious Society of Friends we turn our attention to loving all life: ourselves, others, and the natural world. Being alive becomes praying without ceasing, staying relaxed and non-anxious in this current time and place, and noticing the creative, healing, regenerative movement of the Living Spirit. Our sense of that mysterious, creative Source of all Life in all life convinces us.

Note: In this original Quaker insight, the second coming did not refer to another individual. It referred to "the rising of the Christ within" that raises up the good, true, and loving, and illuminates the cruel, false, and unloving within ourselves, others, and our societies. That every person is a Child of God with a direct experience of the Living Spirit. That we should strive to be our perfect, authentic part of the perfect, divine whole. Many were incarcerated for blasphemy when Friends explained their commitment to the rising of the Christ within themselves and each of us.

Quakers experience the Living Spirit that speaks to our human condition. When we meet the Spirit during times when we are humbled and brought down low, we find conviction.

## Conviction

The word conviction comes from 'convicted.' When we fall short, fail, make mistakes, feel inadequate, or become the perpetrator, we experience the Spirit in a whole new way beyond our own egos. Many traditions see mistakes or failings as the cracks through which God comes. Mistakes allow us to learn. Weaknesses allow us to need others in genuine ways that create community. Failings allow us to experience unequivocal and unconditional love and grace of Life. Without a sense of Spirit in hard times, we experience failings as humiliation that wounds our egos and leads to violence, retribution, and revenge. With a sense of the Spirit in hard times, we find humility, compassion, and conviction. This is a very different experience of the Spirit than in the glorious or all-is-well times.

Some shortcomings arise from wounds that may turn into distress patterns and frozen needs that lead to reliving or reenacting our unresolved pain and unmet needs. Today we better understand how these effects of trauma may lead to cycles of violence, greed, control, envy, egotism, idolatry, hatred, strife, seduction, or addiction. Trauma sets in when we feel our needs outstrip our resources. We feel overwhelmed and freeze, especially when we feel caught alone. When we can experience the Spirit in these moments, we sense the endless resource of the Spirit. We are much less apt to feel overwhelmed and alone, and so less apt to experience trauma. This full awareness of the Spirit heals us and makes us resilient to trauma. The attention of spiritual companions contradicts the isolation, and thus heals. And taking action to express our inward experience in outward form keeps us from freezing and thereby helps us become resilient to trauma.

John Woolman (1763) speaks of the healing power of universal love and our part in lessening each other's distresses, "Our gracious Creator cares and provides for all his creatures. His tender mercies are over all his works; and so far as his love influences our minds, so far we become interested in his workmanship and feel a desire to take hold of every opportunity to lessen the distresses of the afflicted and increase the happiness of the creation. Here we have a prospect of one common interest from which our own is inseparable, that to turn all the treasures we possess into the channel of universal love becomes the business of our lives…"

Other shortcomings arise when we suffer or feel lost, unloved, afraid, mistreated, neglected, or abused, at any age, but especially when we were young. To heal, we have to be ready to heal. We may not be ready to give up our pain, heal, or forgive ourselves or others. But when we are ready, we often cannot do it alone. We need the support of others and the power and healing grace of the Spirit.

Quaker practice is not a formula. We open to the very real, palpable Inward Power of life itself — to create, love, heal, nurture, and transform. Live in the power of the Living Spirit. Learn from mistakes. Offer strengths. Show compassion and mercy, while standing up for ecological and social justice. Robert Barclay (1648–1690) describes a mature Quaker community, "For, when I came into the silent assemblies of God's people, I felt a secret power among them, which touched my heart; and as I gave way unto it I found the evil weakening in me and the good raised up; and so I became thus knit and united unto them, hungering more and more after the increase of this power and life…."

Quaker practice is not a set of beliefs or values. It's a practice that grows from the direct experience of experimenting with the Spirit working in our lives. It's ironic that through failings, mistakes, and pain along with the glorious and all-is-well moments, the Spirit can heal us. Then we see life as beautiful, joyful, and uplifting, and we become a cheerful, energetic, loving people.

## Chapter 4

⌒

# *Activities to*
# *Experience the Living Spirit*

This chapter describes activities to develop our sense of confidence and conviction in the presence of the Living Spirit in our Lives: drawing our core selves, journaling, companion groups, and worship sharing on relevant queries.

### *Draw One's Core Self*

Gather plain white paper and oil pastels or crayons. Ask everyone to relax, and remember a time when you felt totally yourself—alive and engaged, curious, compassionate, creative, and connected. Notice the feeling of one's core self or the Living Spirit in you. If someone says they never felt it, invite them to imagine how it would feel if you did. Draw the feeling. Start with your non-dominant hand and switch hands as you draw. Draw the colors, movements, textures of the feeling, not 'a picture.' When finished, write your name and three words on your picture, any words anywhere you wish. Invite each person to read their name and three words and then tape their drawing on the wall side-by-side. This represents each of us, but also us as a community. This is the place of the Light Within, the place from which to think, make decisions, and take action. When tension or distress arises, ask others to stop, discharge emotion, and consider how to get back to our core selves before proceeding. Posting and pointing to the pictures often helps. If you leave the pictures up in the meetinghouse, anyone may add to or change their drawing any time.


## *Reflect on Convincement*

Gather for about two hours. You can plan for 1.5 - 2.5 hours. Handout and/or post the queries for the session:

- How do I experience the Living Spirit?
- How am I tendered by this Inward Grace? Can I notice when I'm rigid and soften in my body, mind, thoughts, feelings, soul, or spirit?
- How do I let love abide in me, turn to love, and feel loved and loving towards others and nature?
- What do I need to bring into my life or let go of to feel the sacramental wholeness of life in every moment?

Invite the group to address these same queries in three ways:

- *Solo Journal Writing.* Set the time anywhere from 15-30 minutes; we often use 20 minutes.
- *Companion Groups* for 45 minutes. Rotate attention with two people 20 minutes each, three people 13 minutes each, or four people 10 minutes each.
- *Worship Sharing* with the whole group. Set the time anywhere from for 30-75 minutes; we often use 40 or more minutes.


## *Companion Groups on Conviction*

Gather for 45 minutes in groups of two to four people: two people 20 minutes each; three people 12 minutes each; or four people 10 minutes each. Seek clarity and revelation for yourself on the query. Don't try to explain or describe it to others until you become clear within yourself: *How do I experience the Living Spirit when I fall short, fail, make mistakes, feel inadequate, or become the perpetrator?* Come back to the whole group to reflect afterwards: What did you notice? How did that feel? What did you learn? Did it deepen your sense of conviction in the presence and power of the Living Spirit?

## *Reflect on Conviction*

Gather for about two hours. You can plan for 1.5 - 2.5 hours. Handout and/or post the queries for the session:

- How does the Living Spirit speak to my human condition? Do I share my true condition and experiences with other Friends?
- What weakness could I recognize in myself and ask for the help of others?
- How do I suffer? Am I ready to let go and heal? From whom can I ask for help?
- Can I value myself when I fail, become dependent on others, or make mistakes? Do I realize that I do not actually value the life of others who are suffering, if I cannot value myself when I am suffering? Can I give up my fear or terror of failing, becoming dependent on others, or making mistakes?
- Does my lifestyle draw me away from the degenerative, and into a good, whole life?

Invite the group to address these same queries in three ways:

- *Solo Journal Writing.* Set the time anywhere from 15-30 minutes; we often use 20 minutes.
- *Companion Groups* for 45 minutes. Rotate attention with two people 20 minutes each, three people 12 minutes each, or four people 10 minutes each.
- *Worship Sharing* with the whole group. Set the time anywhere from for 30-75 minutes; we often use 40 or more minutes.

~

*It is a bold and colossal claim that we put forward –*
*that the whole of life is sacramental,*
*that there are innumerable 'means of grace'*
*by which God is revealed and communicated –*
*through nature and through human fellowship and through*
*a thousand things that may become the*
*'outward and visible sign' of*
*'an inward and spiritual grace'.*
~ A. Barratt Brown, 1932

~

# Chapter 5

~

# *Experiment with the Living Spirit*

*Quakers experience the Living Spirit
that speaks to our human condition and
we yield to the Spirit to shape and guide our lives.*

## Conversion of Manners

George Fox's famous opening was that we have a direct relationship with the Living Spirit. He wrote (1647), "Thus, when God doth work, who shall (hinder) it? And this I knew experimentally." Quakers come to know the Spirit through experimentation in our lives as well as direct experience. As we change, we notice what we need to have or let go of to stay aware of the Living Spirit in every moment and everything. Then we reflect our inward experience in outward form. This puts our lives in order in ways that make us available and prepared, if or when we are called.

In 1841, at age 21, Caroline Fox wrote in her journal: "Live up to the light thou hast, and more will be granted thee." This proves true. Love and conscience do not spring forth fully formed, they grow as we pay attention to them. One of the primary greetings was, "How is truth prospering in your parts?" I like to ask, "How are love and truth prospering in your parts?" To do this, we use our best discernment. Discernment is our human ability to comprehend the inner nature and relationships of things, especially when obscure, that leads us to keen insight and judgment. Quaker practice is not a blind faith. We test our discernment:

### *Tests of Discernment*

- Sense of the Spirit, life's transforming power, flowing within.
- Persistence in silence, stillness and solitude.
- Simplicity, seemingly trivial or impossible, not willful or desired.
- Integrity: honesty, authenticity and consistency.
- Articulation in personal journal writing and to companions.
- Reflection and feedback from companions.
- Recorded in community, regional, and societal gatherings.
- Documented in the texts of other communities of conscience.
- Expressed in writing, art, news, courts and law.
- Experience of the fruits: love, joy, peace, strength, compassion, beauty, truth, equality and liberty.

William Penn commented on early Friends, "They were changed men themselves before they went about to change others. Their hearts were rent as well as their garments, and they knew the power and work of God upon them... And as they freely received what they had to say from the Lord, so they freely administered it to others. The bent and stress of their ministry was conversion to God, regeneration and holiness..." (Britain Yearly Meeting Faith and Practice 19.48)

In the conversion of manners, how do we distinguish between distress and inspiration? Distress cannot stop and does not respond to external feedback, but inspiration can stop and delights in external feedback. So our primary tests are: 1) the ability to stop, hence silence in Meeting for Worship, and 2) the ability to accept external feedback, hence testimony in Monthly Meeting. We stop and listen plainly to where words and actions come from, and we exchange feedback, speaking plainly to our truth in love without fear. In this manner, each Friend is changed. As Isaac Pennington said, "For this is the true ground of love and unity, not that such a man walks and does just as I do, but because I feel the same Spirit and life in him."

All Friends testimonies reflect one central testimony: to yield to the Spirit to shape and guide our lives. We record insights in our journals and test them with our companions and in our local monthly meetings. Local monthly meetings affirm testimony or insights on faith and practice. They take these to regional or yearly meetings to test with other Friends' meetings. They record what they affirm, and this then informs individuals. When output becomes input it creates regenerative cycles, a living organism, a living experiment with the Spirit in our lives.

Note: We draw on our capacity for love, to feel a tender affection towards and a sense of the preciousness of another person or an element of nature. But love must acknowledge the heart-wrenching reality of being free to leave without ill judgment or retribution—life is infinite, eternal, yet transitory.

We also draw on our capacity for conscience, an inner knowledge of right and wrong with an inward drive to do what is right or regenerative. But conscience must acknowledge the disturbing reality of how difficult it is for us to distinguish between inspiration and woundedness.

Love and conscience go hand-in-hand. As John Woolman (1763) noted, "universal love becomes the business of our lives...." He also said, "Love was the first motion, and then a concern arose...." Whenever truth telling feels harsh, soften and align with the loving heartbeat of that which is true.

*∼*

*... be a terror to all the adversaries of God,*
*and a dread, answering that of God in them all,*
*spreading the Truth...*

*∼ George Fox (1647)*

*∼*

## Chapter 6

⁓

# Activities to Experiment with the Living Spirit

This chapter describes a way to form ongoing Spiritual Companion Groups that support the ongoing experiment with the Spirit in your life. This experiment looks so different in each person's life, we gain a much richer view of the work of the Spirit in our lives when we witness it in the lives of others, too. It also describes a way to reflect on our own personal transformation. Do not forget the essential Quaker practices of worship sharing, keeping a log or journal, and Friendly Faith and Practice Study Queries. You may use any of these as activities as well.

## Form Ongoing Spiritual Companion Groups

You may form ongoing groups of people committed to experiencing the Living Spirit that speaks to our human condition and allows it to shape and guide our lives. Yield to the nudging of love and truth within you. Reflect, think, and act. Then celebrate its joys and fruit. The experience of doing this differs entirely from thinking about doing.

*Spiritual Companion Groups*

- *Meet* every 1-3 weeks with 2-4 people committed to experimenting with the Spirit in daily life.
- *Keep a log* of your experiment, tests of discernment, and feedback.
- *Listen* to where the words come from, stay relaxed and non-anxious in the Spirit in you, and remember the goodness and capabilities of the Spirit in others.
- *Receive* the attention of others in turn: sit silently, listen inwardly, discharge emotion, and/or speak to your spiritual experience, experiment, or to a question or topic.
- *Ask* your companions to reflect back in your words what they heard and/or to offer feedback on guidance you've found.
- *Document* what's affirmed as true for yourself and what is affirmed for others or for all.

*Spiritual Companion Group Questions*

- How do I experience the Living Spirit in easy and difficult times?
- What do I need to have or let go of to stay aware of the Spirit in every moment?
- What distresses do I need to notice, learn from, and discharge?
- What direction has come to me for myself or for us as a culture?
- How are love and conscience shaping and guiding my life?
- What has the Living Spirit revealed to me?
- How can I use what I need and share the rest?
- On whom do I rely? Who relies on me? How do I ask for or offer help?
- With whom do I need to settle disputes?
- What fruits has this experiment borne in my private and public life?

Towards the end of a person's time, invite them to get quiet, notice what guidance is working in them, then listen. If the person finds guidance, they may state it briefly and ask the others to reflect back what they heard. Sometimes that stirs new inner reflection and work. If the guidance remains stable, they may restate it and ask the companions to offer feedback. Companions offer feedback on one thing: whether the listener senses the life and power of the Spirit in the speaker. It does not matter if you like it, agree with it, or even understand it. The question is whether you sense the Spirit in it. Document the feedback of companions as information, not as judgement.


## *Reflect on Personal Transformation*

Gather for about two hours. You can plan for 1.5 - 2.5 hours. Handout and/or post the queries for the session:
- What do I need to have or let go of to stay aware of the Spirit and put my life in order so I'm available if called?
- How is the Spirit shaping and guiding my life, in small and large ways?
- How are love and truth prospering in my life?

Invite the group to address these same queries in three ways:
- *Solo Journal Writing.* Set the time anywhere from 15-30 minutes; we often use 20 minutes.
- *Companion Groups* for 45 minutes. Rotate attention with two people 20 minutes each, three people 12 minutes each, or four people 10 minutes each.
- *Worship Sharing* with the whole group. Set the time anywhere from for 30-75 minutes; we often use 40 or more minutes.

Each part of the session—journaling, companion groups, and worship sharing—address the same queries.

~

*To be afraid is to*
*behave as if the truth*
*were not true...*
*~ Bayard Rustin, 1963*

*We cannot remain honest unless*
*we are opposed to injustice*
*wherever it occurs,*
*first of all in ourselves.*
*~ Bayard Rustin, 1948*

~

*Part III*

~

# *RELIGIOUS SOCIETY*

~

*Oppression in the extreme appears terrible:*
*but oppression in more refined appearances*
*remains to be oppression;*
*and where the smallest degree of it is cherished*
*it grows stronger and more extensive.*
*To labour for a perfect redemption from this spirit of*
*oppression is the great business of the*
*whole family of Christ Jesus in this world.*
~ *John Woolman, 1763*

~

# Chapter 7

~

# *Essential Quaker Structures*

*"...dispatch business quickly, and keep out of long debates and heats; and with the Spirit of God keep that down which is doating about questions and strife of words... but, as the apostles saith, 'be swift to hear, and slow to speak;' and let it be in the grace which seasons all words."* ~ George Fox to the Six Weeks' Meeting in London, Kingston-upon-Thames, 1690

## *An Ecology of Practice*

Quaker practice is mystical, but not laissez-faire, fanatical, or a call to blind faith. It's our direct experience of and experiment with the Spirit in our lives.

The Spirit transforms individuals. Individuals testify to their insights and transformations in the Monthly Meeting where other individuals affirm their best sense of what rings true. Everyone learns from everyone else's testimony. Sometimes we find that the testimony of one person is essential for others, too. When something is recognized as essential for everyone in the Monthly Meeting, we record it as a testimony of the meeting. That testimony is then shared with neighboring meetings to be tested in the Quarterly or Yearly Meeting. Then the Quarterly or Yearly Meeting affirms their best sense of what rings true for a specific meeting. Meetings learn from each other, and sometimes find the testimony of one meeting is essential for other meetings also. When it is recognized as essential for everyone in the Yearly Meeting, we record a new corporate testimony in our Faith and Practice. The Faith and Practice becomes guidance to individuals to shape our lives that brings discernment full circle. This self-referential cycle creates a regenerative ecology of practice.

A Quaker community reflects the measure of individual Friends' faith, practice, and integrity. Individuals are the channel of spiritual revelation. Individual Friends also reflect the measure of the Meeting's faith, practice, and integrity. We grow in relation to our Meeting's capacity for feedback and discernment. Just another way of acknowledging the self-referential cycle that creates this ecology of practice.

In this way, the whole meeting is set on a course for a more vital and fruitful faith. Too often, to avoid conflict, to comfort Friends arriving with a faith trauma in their past, or to avoid facing theological differences, a meeting adapts its identity to the vaguest version of faith and practice in its circle, Quaker or not. Then, the vision becomes blurry, the faith becomes tepid, and the witness becomes muzzled or defused.

Membership is recognized by the Monthly Meeting, but we become a member of the Yearly Meeting under the discipline of that Faith and Practice. When we see the Yearly Meeting as a religious society of the total membership of every Friend in every Monthly Meeting, then Documents in Advance for Annual Sessions become essential. We send Documents in Advance to every Monthly Meeting enough in advance so that every Friend can reflect on them in themselves and their meeting community to bring the best discernment of the entire membership to the Sessions.

When I was young, my family dedicated one day a week to the Monthly Meeting, and other opportunities as they arose, and one weekend a month to the business of the Quarterly and Yearly Meeting. They lived their faith in the community; they didn't talk about it. It was a beautiful, powerful community. But when I moved away, I had no language to describe Quakerism, what "it" was, or how "it" was done.

# An Ecology of Quaker Practice

The Living Spirit
in All Life

Yearly Meeting
for Worship & Business
Societal Witness
Community Formation

Meeting

Meeting

Meeting

Monthly Meeting
for Worship & Business
Testimony & Community Witness
Individual Formation Minutes

Companions
Healing &
Discernment

Individual
Experiment, Study
Personal Witness
Household Formation
Journals

Advices and Queries
Faith and Practice

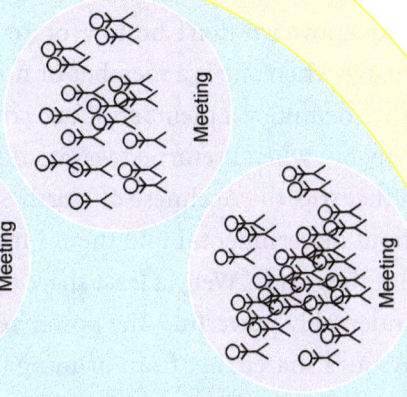

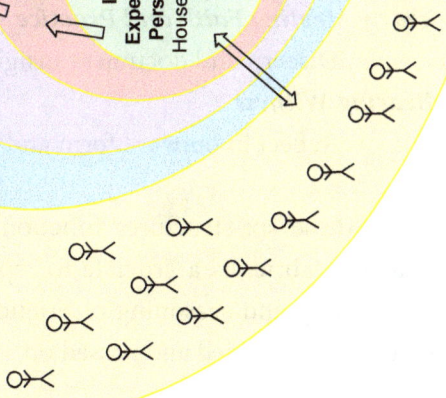

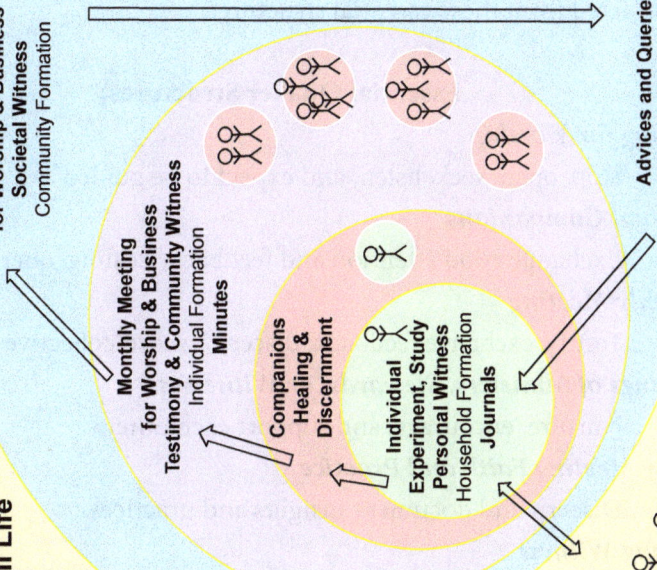

Witness
through relationships
with others and the
natural world
and through
public record.

I had lived it, but with all my experience, I could not explain or recreate it in a new place. I worked for decades to get clear about the essential elements. I tried nearly full-time for three years but failed. So I wrote to my Meeting to lay down my membership. But my meeting said, "You know we don't bestow or revoke membership, we can only acknowledge when one is a member or not, and we're sorry to inform you, but you are definitely a member of our community." They said I should go on my trip, but when I returned we should discuss what was going on with this. On that trip, the Acehnese of North Sumatra asked me to share what I knew about discernment. I told them I had been working on that and had failed. But they said, "Well, at least share the things you know." When I did, it was undeniably powerful. The power seemed to stem not only from the few activities I shared, but from pruning the other activities that obscured or distracted from these essential structures:

### Essential Quaker Structures

*Meeting for Worship*
>  Stop, open, seek, listen, and expect to be guided as a people.

*Spiritual Companions*
>  Exchange good attention and feedback, healing, queries, insight.

*Monthly Meeting*
>  Testify, exchange feedback, discern, record collective testimonies.

*Meetings of Ministers, Stewards, or Witnesses*
>  Nurture, encourage, and support each other.

*Yearly Meeting Faith and Practice*
>  Discern and document insights and practices.

*Bearing Witness*
>  Reflect in outward form and enter in public record.

These six structures function as one interdependent, spiritually-dynamic fabric, as a crucible for spiritual transformation within which the shaping and seasoning of Friends' faith and practice is revealed and matures, is recorded and passed on.

## *Meeting for Worship*

The first structure of the Religious Society of Friends, Meeting for Worship is so simple and yet amazingly complex. In Meeting for Worship we stop. Stop in your body and in your mind. Your brain is a muscle. Feel it soften inside your skull. Let go and open to the Spirit. Don't sit in Meeting for Worship with an habitual guard up, just to rest and build up enough energy to go back and live a stressed or distressing life. Let your guard down, which can feel awkward or even terrifying. Let everything go and open yourself to the Spirit. This is a very physical practice of the orientation of every cell in your body.

When we're inwardly guided, a primary test of whether we are acting out of inspiration or distress is the ability to stop -- distress does not want to stop. So the stopping and letting go is an important part of the way we open to the Living Spirit. In that open space, we can listen inwardly to the still, small voice nudging within, the truth working within us. You can let go of the distress, and go quietly inside to touch that truth within you that's not aligned with your life, and expect to receive revelation and guidance, for yourself and for us as a people.

If a message comes to you for yourself, do not share it, let it work within you. Write it in your journal and work on the implications for yourself. If it rings true, you might be excited about sharing it, but often once you share it you feel like you're done, that's it. But that's NOT it. You need to take the revelation inside, write it down, experiment with it, try it, test it, and let it work on you and change you. Then share the revelation and how it has changed you with your companion(s), and maybe with your community.

If a message comes to you for others or for us as a people, stand and speak it out to deliver it. We are the channel through which revelation comes. So when you feel moved, it's your responsibility to stand and speak. Whether it comes to you during the week and the message is prepared or spontaneous, whether before, during, or after formal worship time, part of worship is to deliver to your community the revelation and messages that arise out of worship.

Meeting for Worship is a practice of both plain listening and of plain speaking. But it's not our job to "get" messages. It's our job to receive them when they come. But as Quakers, it's our primary job to celebrate the Spirit with gratitude. Be whole, be well, and delight in the gift of life. Live in and draw strength from a real, present, palpable power of the Spirit. In this pure joy, we can be fully aware of the source of our emotions or distresses, our rage or outrage, but we do not fuel them or let them fuel us. We draw our strength and power from the Spirit of life. We enter Meeting for Worship to practice the physical work of fully entering into our celebration of life, yielding into its nature, allowing the truth to change me, and breathing in a sense of wholeness, gratitude, and joy, just delighting in the gift of life.

Then extend that sense of worship into every moment of our lives, a kind of praying without ceasing, appreciating and celebrating life in every moment. Treat daily life as a sacrament, focused on what is loving and true in every moment. Stop and worship at the start and end of each day. Look for opportunities to gather with others, daily or weekly, to let go, open to the Spirit, and expect to receive guidance. After worship, note in your journal any revelation or messages that spoke to you, then act on them, and bring them to speak to your companions and potentially to the Monthly Meeting to test.

### Meeting for Worship
Gather and settle into silence.
Stop, let go, and open to the Living Spirit.
Listen inwardly, expect the Spirit to heal and guide us.
Let messages for myself work within me.
Stand and speak messages for the community.
Close with greeting and visitation.

## *Spiritual Companions*

Spiritual Companions was the second structure of the Religious Society of Friends, none better known than the Valiant Sixty. Quakers often lived, worked, and traveled in pairs.

When we're inwardly guided, the two primary tests of whether we are acting out of inspiration or distress is the ability to stop and to accept external feedback—distress cannot stop and does not respond to external feedback. I talked about how important stopping is in the section on Meeting for Worship. With our spiritual companions, we share our experiment, ask for feedback, say "thank you," and imagine if what they say was true.

Spiritual companions are pairs or small groups of people, we usually are 2-4 people, who are mutually committed to experimenting with the Spirit in private and public life. They meet regularly (every 1-3 weeks) for however long the group chooses. The group divides up the time equally to give each person good attention in turn.

A good companion is a good listener who stops in body and mind, turns towards the person speaking, follows what they are saying with curiosity, and imagines if what they were saying were true. In addition to being a good listener, a good companion stays relaxed and non-anxious in their core self, or in the Spirit, and remembers the goodness and capability of the speaker in their core self, or the Spirit in them.

Work with companions is varied and rich. We come to see the experiment with the Spirit in each person's life and affirm these variations without putting certain ones up or down. We simply divide the time equally and give each person time with good attention. When it's my time, I ask myself, "What do I need?" Settle into silence, contemplation, and prayer, opening to healing or guidance. Describe how I experience the Spirit in easy, glorious times and in hard times, when I fall short, feel inadequate, fail or am the perpetrator. Discharge the emotion out of my body--cry, tremble, cry out, laugh, emote. Let my mind clear and open to insights and direction. Or I can share the fruits of experimenting with the Spirit in my life. Identify insights, directions or queries that guide me, and test them with the others by asking for their feedback.

When we test with others, there is only one question, "Can you feel the life and power of the Spirit in it?" Or, "Do you sense that it rings true?" If not, give it more time. If so, record this feedback in your journal. If it rings true for others too, record it in the Companion Group's journal and take it to the community. The community then gives the group feedback. If it's true for the whole community, they then record that as a new testimony, insight, or practice. This guidance inspires others to greater faithfulness. So with the Meeting for Worship and Spiritual Companions we have this grounding in the ability to stop and receive external feedback which is critical to our commitment to being inwardly guided.

### *Companion Groups*

- Gather and settle into silence.
- Take equal time in turn to reflect on the experiment with the Spirit in your life.
- Companions stay relaxed and non-anxious in the Spirit, and focus on the Spirit in the speaker.
- During your time, you may:
  - Be still and listen inwardly.
  - Discharge emotions.
  - Speak on your experiment with the Spirit, or to the guides or questions.
  - Yield to the nudgings of love and truth within you.
- Preserve time, if desired, to formulate testimony of faith or practice. If so:
  - Ask your companion(s) to reflect back what they heard in your words. You may sense the need for more work, or feel increased confidence in your testimony. If the latter:
  - Ask your companion(s) to offer feedback on whether they sense the Spirit in it.
- Document in your journal any testimony, reflections, or feedback.
- Bring testimonies that ring true for all of you to the Monthly Meeting.

- Close the meeting after everyone has a turn, and the group has settled.
- Act between meetings, and celebrate the joys and fruits of the Spirit.

You may begin with or review occasionally the questions on being Available and Prepared.

### *Available and Prepared*

- Am I taking care of myself: my health, sleep, water, food, activity, curiosity, tranquility, balance?
- Is my heart open? Is there grief, fear, anger, apathy, joy, delight, gratitude I need to discharge?
- Is my mind open? Is there confusion, insight, understanding, integrity I need to notice?
- Is my conscience open? Am I listening inwardly, growing, learning, experimenting, changing?
- Do I love life and act on what I know to be true, for the joy of it, as a life commitment?
- Do I record what I know to be true in public record: writing, art, music, law, court, news, curriculum, etc?
- Am I living in integrity with life's transforming power?

Later you may wish to speak to any one or more of the Companion Group Questions.

### *Companion Group Questions*

- How do I experience the Living Spirit in my private and public life?
- What do I need to have or let go of to stay aware of the Spirit in every moment?
- What distresses do I need to notice, learn from, and discharge?
- Who do I rely on? Who relies on me? How do I ask for or offer help?
- How do love and conscience shape and guide my life?
- What has the Living Spirit revealed to me?
- How can I use what I need and share the rest?
- What direction has come to me for myself or for us as a culture?
- With whom do I need to settle disputes?
- What fruits has this experiment borne in my private and public life?

## Monthly Meeting

Monthly Meeting was the third structure of the Religious Society of Friends to add discipline to our faith and practice. Because the Spirit is universal and recognizable by others, especially those who commit to spiritual life, a significant test of discernment among Friends was to gather monthly to testify to how they were being changed and guided by the Spirit and receive feedback from others. Monthly Meeting is a uniquely Quaker practice.

This work of personal testifying, asking for and receiving feedback, and documenting our testimony changes us, both individually and as a society. The nature of that change in us changes what we bring to and how we approach discernment on collective matters and the settlement of community disputes. So start with personal testimony on:

- What you need to have or to let go of to stay aware of and grounded in the Spirit.
- How the Spirit is guiding and changing you--insights or practices that are shaping your life.
- How the Spirit, through love and conscience, is prospering in your personal and public life.

Then follow Michael Sheeran's observation in *Beyond Majority Rule*: ask if the testimony is clear first, and allow for clarifying questions. Then invite community members to each share their response or feedback, focused on one thing alone: Do you sense the Spirit in it? The question is NOT if you like it, agree with it, or even understand it. The question is: Does it ring true in the speaker? Do you sense the life and power of the Spirit in it? We often don't like or agree with the truth, but it is true. We may not understand, but we can still sense the Spirit moving in it or not. Answering this question simply informs the speaker; it is not judgment.

If the community affirms, then document if the group sensed it rang true for the speaker only, for a few people, or everyone. If the testimony is true for the entire meeting, share it with neighboring meetings. Consider in the quarterly or yearly meeting if it rings true for that one meeting, a few meetings, or everyone. If for everyone, then record it in the Yearly Meeting Faith and Practice. New corporate testimonies emerge naturally as a by-product of this practice of Monthly, Quarterly, and Yearly Meetings.

Then attend to any suffering for love and conscience sake that occur from applying testimonies affirmed by the community in our lives.

After attending to personal testimony or sufferings, then take up the decisions or disputes in the community. Distinguish among decisions that require spiritual discernment, pastoral care or counseling, or just need someone to make the decision or take the action. Openly ask if a matter requires spiritual discernment, pastoral care, or just someone to do it, and sincerely invite input and feedback. Building the skill to make this distinction correctly by many people in the meeting greatly strengthens the Monthly Meeting.

Once an item is clear, then open to the Spirit, listen quietly, and speak honestly — state any simple truths that come to you and trust the Spirit to work within, heal, and guide. Speak to whether you sense the life and power in it that 'rings true'.

An individual may feel so strongly that they wish to stand in the way or stand aside. Then it is the group's responsibility to stop and explore the truth in their concern and be changed by it. If the sense of the Meeting is unchanged, it's the obligation of the group to say so, with loving tenderness, and to move ahead. Do not allow an individual to "hold a meeting hostage." If appropriate, record the concerns of anyone who objects or stands aside. It may help the group to understand when troubles arise later.

So in the Monthly Meeting attend to personal testimony of how the Spirit is working in our lives first, and then attend to meeting concerns or disputes that require spiritual discernment. This will result in generating new corporate testimonies for us as a people today.

### Monthly Meeting

- Settle into silence.
- Read personal testimonies first, one-by-one.
- Ask "Is it clear or unclear?" Clarify as needed.
- Do you sense the Spirit in it, that it 'rings true', not if you like, agree with or understand it.
  - If no, say so. Let the person respond. If still no, the person accepts that feedback.
  - If yes, record it in the community book with the person's name and words.
- Ask "Is it true for others?" If so, add their names; if everyone, record it as a corporate testimony.
- Then read community decisions, directions, or settlements of disputes, one-by-one.
- Ask "Is it clear or unclear?" Clarify as needed.
- Speak to your sense of the Living Spirit in it.
- After everyone has a chance to speak, then speak again if you have a new revelation.
- When a sense of unity or a resonant collection of threads emerges, name and record that.
- Leave a moment of silence after each agenda item, then move to the next.

## Meetings of Ministers, Stewards, or Witnesses

Meetings of Ministers, Stewards, or Witnesses began as the Seventh Day meeting of ministers and elders, and later the meeting of overseers. Much later these evolved into the committee structure familiar to us today. Ministry and Worship or Ministry and Counsel focuses on ministry and our inward lives. Stewardship, Nurture, or Oversight focuses on stewardship and our outward lives. Witness or Peace and Social Concerns, which today includes Earth care witness, focuses on witness and our public lives.

In each of these aspects of our faith and practice, Quakers balance two different dichotomies:

1. Applying the implications of spiritual guidance  to both our personal and public lives.
2. Listening for both what we need to have, create, or act on as well as let go of, resist, or oppose.

Being guided by the Living Spirit, rather than theory or ideology, allows us to focus on our whole lives, personal and public, and our whole selves, when we say yes or no. This is so simple we can miss the fact that this is quite unique, and contributes to the compelling nature of Quaker witness historically.

Friends are known for their yea is their yea, and their nay is their nay. I thought of this as truth telling, that Quakers were honest. But as I apply my best discernment of spiritual guidance throughout my life, I come to recognize things that may appear to be bad but in truth are good, and what may appear to be good but in truth are bad. When we do this, others see us doing this. Then they come to ask for our feedback on what things truly are, regenerative, loving, and conscientious or not, what is of the Spirit and what is not.

Quakers laid down the laity, because we each committed to this practice spiritual discernment throughout our whole lives. We each grow in our ministry, stewardship, and witness. At times we may choose to spend more time on one aspect of our faith and practice, or certain people may have gifts in a certain area. So some people may take a turn as a member, while others may spend a good portion of their lives in one or another of these groups. In our membership in any one of these groups, we commit to:

- Tend and nurture that aspect of our own lives, thereby teaching or witnessing by example.
- Get to know each member of the meeting in that aspect of their life, and seek ways to nurture, encourage, and provide resources for each of them.
- Get to know the meeting as a whole, us as a people, and what the meeting needs in this aspect.

When each of these groups meets, typically monthly, the group attends to a number of perspectives:

- Worship sharing or spiritual companion sharing on our own experience.
- Share what we have come to know about or done to support each individual in the meeting.
- Share our sense of the meeting and what we as a community need to grow.
- Seek guidance and test discernment, or season specific matters that arise in the meeting.

It's in approaching the work as tending ourselves, each other, and us as a people that weaves the spiritual community and the Religious Society of Friends.

### Meetings of Ministers, Stewards, or Witnesses

- Commit to living out Quaker faith and practice in our lives.
- Get to know each member and the meeting as a whole in this aspect of our lives.
- Offer encouragement, nurture, and resources to individuals and to the community in this aspect of our lives.
- Meet regularly, typically monthly, to attend to this aspect of our faith and practice:
- Worship sharing or spiritual companion sharing on ourselves.
- Share what we have come to know about or done to support each individual in the meeting.
- Share our sense of the meeting and what we as a community need to grow.
- Seek guidance, season, and test discernment on specific matters that arise.

## Yearly Meeting Faith and Practice

Yearly Meeting Faith and Practice is the Book of Discipline that guides individual Quakers. Monthly Meetings may acknowledge when someone has become a member, but their membership is in the Religious

Society, including the monthly, quarterly, and yearly meeting.

The Yearly Meeting Faith and Practice grows out of individuals seeking and experimenting with the Spirit in their lives. The Gospel has no covers, our lives are the gospel text. We continue to receive revelation on the nature and movement of the Spirit among us.

A good experiment needs a log, what we call a journal, to track, test, and record the fruit of the experiment. Ask and it will be given to you; seek and you will find; knock and the door will be opened to you. (Matthew 7:7; Luke 11:9) Friends ask, seek, and knock, and we document in our journals what is given, what we find, and how the way opens, tested by our companions.

Monthly Meetings document the discernment of the meeting membership in their book of Minutes. We record testimonies affirmed by the meeting with the person(s) name, and new corporate testimonies when something is affirmed by the whole Monthly Meeting.

Yearly Meetings document the discernment of the society in their book of Minutes. We record testimonies affirmed by the Yearly Meeting with the meeting(s) name, and new corporate testimonies affirmed by the whole society. Significant statements of faith or practice are selected for the Faith and Practice, including Advices and Queries. This in turn educates and guides individual Quakers. Meeting members may use the Friendly Faith and Practice Study queries to study the Faith and Practice texts.

This self-referential cycle creates a self-organizing society based on discernment. But this requires that the people value and engage in the Spirit in our lives and this cycle of discernment, and prune away other distractions. When Yearly Meeting truly engages in this cycle, Documents in Advance become essential for the entire membership to read and seek clarity on as a Monthly Meeting, and to bring that clarity and insight to the Quarterly and Yearly Meetings. This simple cycle is increasingly rare, yet a powerful way to bring the Beloved Community and Religious Society to life.

## Bearing Witness

Bearing Witness to the Living Spirit. Substance offers the most primary structure to our lives. When older and young people work together, we do not organize around "whatever-the-adult-says", nor should we organize around "whatever-the-child-wants". We organize around the love and truth of a matter, which provides its own structure. That is why Quakers speak plainly, and do not elaborate, defend, or persuade, but to lay out the truth as best we sense it and let the love and truth of the matter work on us.

What witness is sometimes seems difficult to pin down for many reasons.

We witness in several ways, through our outward forms that reflect our inward experience; our loving, conscientious relationships with others and the natural world; and the fruit of our lives: love, joy, peace, strength, compassion, beauty, truth, equality, and liberty.

Witness also has two sides: illuminating, resisting, and opposing all that is contrary to the Spirit, or degenerative, as well as following and yielding into the direction of the Spirit, or regenerative. Most human activities focus on one or the other, not both simultaneously. So it's not a pattern of cooperative thinking and action that feels ordinary.

Witness is also very challenging. As Quakers we love to think of walking cheerfully over the world, answering that of God in every one. But the full quote from George Fox is a bit more challenging and demanding. It also fluidly mixes elements of opposing that which is contrary and calling out that which is of the Spirit (1656): "In the power of life and wisdom, and dread of the Lord God of life, and heaven, and earth, dwell; that in the wisdom of God over all ye may be preserved, and be a terror to all the adversaries of God, and a dread, answering that of God in them all, spreading the Truth abroad, awakening the witness, confounding deceit, gathering up out of transgression into the life, the covenant of light and peace with God. Let all nations hear the word by sound or writing. Spare no place, spare not tongue nor pen, but be obedient to the Lord God and go through the world and be valiant for the Truth upon earth; tread and trample all that is contrary under. ...And this is... a charge to you all in the presence of the living God: be patterns, be examples in all countries, places, islands, nations, wherever you come, that your carriage and life may preach among all sorts of people, and to them; then you will come to walk cheerfully over the world, answering that of God in every one."

I put the emphasis on "then." We do not seek to walk cheerfully over the world, answering that of God in everyone; we seek to yield to the truth in all of it's petty, overwhelming, disruptive, and inconvenient demands in every aspect of our lives. We seek to "act justly and to love mercy and to walk humbly with our God" (Micah 6:8). The truth often is not what we like, agree with, want, or understand. It's uncomfortable to be a terror to the adversaries of God... treading and trampling out all that is contrary. But honestly, that's what a lot of the work of a witness feels like. I often give in or give up and do not hold the course when I get into these white waters.

But even in the most disturbing and distressing human affairs, William Penn (1682) describes, "True godliness don't turn men out of the world, but enables them to live better in it, and excites their endeavours to mend it..." Then, when we yield and rely on the Spirit through all the trials of our lives, and enter our insights into the public record of letters, writings, songs, art, curriculum, law, or court, others turn to us to be witnesses both in day-to-day life or in court. Quakers are committed to creating and following law, unless the law violates our conscience or religious conviction. Then we are obligated to publicly break such laws so that we may enter our testimony into the public court record. Each Quaker is called, in our own ways, to "be patterns, be examples in all countries, places, islands, nations, wherever you come, that your carriage and life may preach among all sorts of people, and to them." (George Fox)

As Friends, we rely on the substance of the Inward Guide and the love and truth of a matter to provide the structure of our lives and communities. When we see the structure created by love and truth itself and our relationships of communion and mutual discernment, we experience a joy, a playfulness and delight, a sense of peace and liberty that is worth all its challenges, and cannot be found through any other means.

~

*They were changed men themselves*
*before they went about to change others.*
*Their hearts were rent*
*as well as their garments,*
*and they knew the power and*
*work of God upon them...*
~ *William Penn*

~

# Chapter 8

⌒

# *Activities to Practice Essential Quaker Structures*

This chapter describes how to use our own core structures as the source of our education. Host each essential structure with special, deliberate attention, reflection, and expression. We learn by combining experience and reflection. This is where the "Ah, ha!" occurs. We also learn by teaching, by finding our voice to express to others what we are doing.

## *Host and Reflect on Quaker Gatherings*

For each essential Quaker gathering, one at a time, read the basic directions and conduct the gathering with a special intention of applying the directions. Then reflect on the experience afterwards.

For Meeting for Worship and Monthly Meeting, gather at the usual time, or schedule a separate time to experiment with how approaching Meeting for Worship with this specific intention changes the experience of meeting. At the beginning of the meeting, read the description from this text, your Faith and Practice, and/or other reference. At the end of the meeting, reflect on the experience.

For Companion Groups and Meetings of Ministers, Stewards, or Witnesses schedule reflection time after companion groups meet every 4-6 months, and rearrange the companion groups at that time.

Notice how the experience of practicing these gatherings is completely different from thinking or talking about doing them. So practice them with initial guidance or reminders. Read the card at the beginning of each gathering. No matter how long people have been doing or hearing it. Reading simple instructions before each gathering guides newcomers and reminds those with experience. Then reflect on the practice to gain insight. We also learn and retain more when we describe, express, or teach others the practice. Follow these steps:

- *Host the practice* at the regular time in your Meeting's schedule, or at a special time.

- *Share the instructions* on cards or a poster for each participant to see. Read the card at the beginning without any added language. "Now we will do _____." [Read the card.]

- *Ask*, "Are we clear?" Answer only questions that require clarification on the practice or content, otherwise say, "Please share that during the process." Keep clarifications to as few words as possible, preserving time for the practice and reflection.

- *Do the practice.*

- *Reflect on the practice* afterwards reserving at least twenty minutes to make sure you get to the last question: "What did you notice?" Or, "What was your experience of that practice?" "What stood out to you about the content?" "What stood out to you about the practice or structure?" People often need to process their personal experience and the content before they can step back and consider the format or approach.

- *Document and publish* the reflection in the Meeting newsletter or Monthly Meeting Minutes, or in art, song, writing, publications, curriculum, law, wherever is appropriate. Invite three adults to lead the practice with children or youth after doing it with adults, or vice versa.

## Conduct Activity Debriefing

Conduct activity debriefings after any meeting event or gathering. Invite people to write implications for themselves in their personal journals (3 minutes), talk in small groups of three on what they experienced or learned (10 minutes), and share implications for us as a culture in the whole group (10 minutes). We used this debriefing at a learning center on nearly every activity and it took 2-3 years for people to get used to the last question on implications for us as a culture and feel they had something worthwhile to share. So be persistent.

## Compile, Use, and Test Monthly Meeting Minutes

Compile, Use, and Test Monthly Meeting Minutes of formative statements of faith or practice. Collect them by decade and study them as a meeting. Submit ones that ring true for your meeting today to your Yearly Meeting to test with other meetings, get feedback, and, if true for others, be added to your Faith and Practice.

## Friendly Faith and Practice Study

We use these queries to study the Bible, other religious texts, or Yearly Meeting Faith and Practice. I adapted the queries slightly from Spears & Spears (1997):

*Friendly Faith and Practice Study*
What are the main points in this passage?
What new light do I find in this particular reading?
How is this passage true to my experience or our experience?
What problems do I have with this text?
What are the implications for my life and for us as a people?

As well as studying your own Yearly Meeting's Faith and Practice, you may study Britain Yearly Meeting's Faith and Practice, or a collection of other Yearly Meetings' Faith and Practice. It's also instructive to look up topics of concern in a variety of Yearly Meeting's Faith and Practices to consider a topic more broadly and deeply. The Faith and Practice is descriptive, not prescriptive.

One should not be quick to discard long-standing teachings, advices, or queries. But insight evolves over time through continuing revelation.

## *Focus Companion Group Sessions on Witness*

Focus companion group Sessions on witness or join a meeting of witnesses to support each other in these steps:

- *Reflect your faith in the Living Spirit in outward form* and in loving, conscientious relationships with others and the natural world. Illuminate, resist, and oppose all that is contrary to the Spirit and degenerative. Follow the wisdom and practice of all that is of the Spirit, or generative.
- *Testify to faith and practice in your daily life* in your monthly meeting, and ask for the meeting's feedback and record for yourself or a few others who join you in that witness. Take testimony that speaks to the whole community to the yearly meeting, and ask for feedback. If other meetings concur, document new corporate testimonies in the Yearly Meeting Faith and Practice.
- *Respond when others turn to you* to test the veracity of a subject, in day-to-day life or in court.
- *Enter into the public record* your insights about our faith and practice in letters, writings, music, art, curriculum, law, or court proceedings.

# *About the Author*

Nadine Hoover is from the Buffalo Friends Meeting in New York Yearly Meeting. She grew up in Alfred Friends Meeting in western New York State. A half dozen Quaker families settled in this small, rural community because they had done alternative service as conscientious objectors to World War II in western New York. Many of them had grown up in Quaker communities and families. They discerned decisions together and let their lives speak, as individuals and a body. They lived out of their Quaker faith and practice, but they did not talk about how they did it. So they did not attract newcomers or teach members how to describe Quaker practice to others.

In her youth, Nadine attended Powell House and Philadelphia work camps. She graduated from George School in 1978 and Friends World College in 1982. Nadine served as Secretary of Southeastern Yearly Meeting, 1997-99, and as Manager of the Friends General Conference Bookstore in 1999. Southeastern Yearly Meeting released her to travel in the ministry in 1996, and New York Yearly Meeting in 1999. She served as Coordinator of Friends Peace Teams in Asia West Pacific, 2007-2018.

Still, Nadine struggled to articulate Quaker practice. After three years of intensive writing, in 2009 she gave up. But Indonesian friends asked her to share what she knew of discernment. So she listed a few key elements. When tried, they blossomed. First, doing them creates a simple regenerative cycle of activity, an ecology of practice. And second, pruning away nonessential elements clears the way to thrive. To reap the benefits, we ask both what we should stop doing and what we should do.

To reap the benefits, we ask both what we should stop doing and what we should do. Then we dedicated to experimenting with the Spirit in our lives. We don't do this alone, we do this with others. So many people are seeking to understand and experience these Quaker practices.

⌣

*To love those called enemies and become friends,*
*so begins the work of peace.*
*~ Nadine Hoover, 2019*

⌣

# References

*N. Jean Toomer quote from:*
Black Fire: African American Quakers on Spirituality and Human Rights
(2011). Edited by Harold D. Weaver, Jr., Paul Kriese, and Stephen W. Angell
with Anne Steere Nash. Philadelphia: Quaker Press of FGC.

*Friendly Faith and Practice Study questions from:*
Spears, Joanne; Spears, Larry (1997). "Friendly Bible Study" www.quak-
ers4re.org/node/143 and "Friendly Faith and Practice Study Guide."
iBooks, QuakerBooks.

*British Quaker quotes from:*
Quaker Faith & Practice: The book of Christian discipline of the Yearly
Meeting of the Religious Society of Friends (Quakers) in Britain, Fifth
edition (2013). https://qfp.quaker.org.uk/

*Special gratitude* for the support of the Thomas H. & Mary Williams
Shoemaker Fund, Philadelphia, PA, the Quaker Religious Education Collaborative, and Friends Peace Teams.

Quakers4re.org • FriendsPeaceTeams.org • Quaker.org
Cultures-of-Peace.org • CourageousGifts.com
AVP.International • RC.org
NWTRCC.org • centeronconscience.org

Published by:
Relentless Publishing House, LLC
www.relentlesspublishing.com

RELENTLESS
PUBLISHING

ISBN: 9781948829700

# ANCHORED

Finding HOPE in the Promises of God

## Dr. Irene E. Watson

RELENTLESS
PUBLISHING

The Bible is the final authority in my life. Regardless of the negative and deleterious comments of some, its biblical principles have withstood the test of time. I read, study, meditate, teach and try to live by its' truths on a daily basis. However, I understand that very few Christians stop to read the scriptures from the Holy Bible for themselves. Very seldom is reflection and meditation the order of the day for many. Unfortunately, few Christians understand that there is power in reading, meditating, and living the Holy Scriptures.

This journal is a mirror image of my love for God and His Word. God's Word strengthens and reassures me that He is always with me in any given situation. I find hope in the scriptures, my joy and expectation are restored as I meditate and reflect on his precious promises.

I wrote this 21-day journal for a reflection of scriptures in order to ignite an excitement of hope in every person who reads it; to petition them to re-examine their hearts and experience God in a new way. My prayer is that this journal will evoke a time of confidence and assurance in God's promises that all things are possible.

I love to inspire, motivate and encourage people by sharing the scriptures. Optimistically, I pray that each of you will sense the love of God and find the strength to lift your head as you apply the Word to your individual situation. I believe that this journal will inspire and motivate you to go deeper in the Word of God, search the scriptures for yourself and stand firm on God's truth.

# Day 1

For I know the plans I have for you, declares the Lord, plans to prosper you and not to harm you, plans to give you hope and a future.

Jeremiah 29:11

# What do you believe God is speaking to your heart concerning this scripture?

_____

_____

_____

_____

_____

_____

_____

_____

_____

_____

_____

_____

_____

_____

_____

_____

_____

_____

# Day 2

So do not fear, for I am with you; do not be dismayed, for I am your God. I will strengthen you and help you; I will uphold you with my righteous right hand.

Isaiah 41:10

# What have you been fearful about? How did knowing God turn your fear into faith?

_____

_____

_____

_____

_____

_____

_____

_____

_____

_____

_____

_____

_____

_____

_____

_____

# *Day 3*

But they that wait upon the Lord shall renew their strength; they shall mount up with wings as eagles; they shall run, and not be weary; and they shall walk, and not faint.

Isaiah 40:31

Have you ever had to wait upon the Lord
for anything?  What does waiting upon
the Lord mean to you? Give examples.

_____

_____

_____

_____

_____

_____

_____

_____

_____

_____

_____

_____

_____

_____

_____

_____

_____

# $\mathcal{D} a y$ 4

Favour is deceitful, and beauty is vain: but a woman that feareth the Lord, she shall be praised.

Proverbs 31:30

What does the fear of the Lord mean
to you? How is the fear of the Lord
different from the fear of man?

_____

_____

_____

_____

_____

_____

_____

_____

_____

_____

_____

_____

_____

_____

_____

# Day 5

Be still, and know that I am
God: I will be exalted among
the heathen, I will be
exalted in the earth.

Psalm 46:10

How would you describe who God is to you? What does it mean to you to be still in the presence of God?

_____

_____

_____

_____

_____

_____

_____

_____

_____

_____

_____

_____

_____

_____

_____

_____

_____

# Day 6

Behold, I stand at the door, and knock: if any man hear my voice, and open the door, I will come in to him, and will sup with him, and he with me.

Revelation 3:20

Have you ever heard the voice of God and not let Him in? If yes, what were the consequences of that situation? If no, explain why it is important to hear and obey.

_____

_____

_____

_____

_____

_____

_____

_____

_____

_____

_____

_____

_____

_____

_____

_____

# *Day* 7

So shall they fear the name of the LORD from the west, and his glory from the rising of the sun. When the enemy shall come in, like a flood the Spirit of the LORD shall lift up a standard against him.

Isaiah 59:19

# What recent battles has the Lord raised up a standard against in your life?

_____

_____

_____

_____

_____

_____

_____

_____

_____

_____

_____

_____

_____

_____

_____

_____

# Day 8

For God so loved the world,
that he gave his only
begotten Son, that
whosoever believeth in him
should not perish, but have
everlasting life.

John 3:16

# What does this scripture say to your heart?

_____

_____

_____

_____

_____

_____

_____

_____

_____

_____

_____

_____

_____

_____

_____

_____

# Day 9

And I will establish my covenant with you, neither shall all flesh be cut off any more by the waters of a flood; neither shall there anymore be a flood to destroy the earth.

Genesis 9:11

# Define covenant and explain why this biblical covenant is important to man.

_____

_____

_____

_____

_____

_____

_____

_____

_____

_____

_____

_____

_____

_____

_____

_____

_____

_____

_____

# Day 10

Give, and it shall be given unto you; good measure, pressed down, and shaken together, and running over, shall men give into your bosom. For with the same measure that ye mete withal it shall be measured to you again.

Luke 6:38 KJV

Explain what to give good measure, pressed down, shaken together and running means to you. How do you live out this promise of giving in your life?

_____

_____

_____

_____

_____

_____

_____

_____

_____

_____

_____

_____

_____

_____

_____

# Day 11

Beloved, now are we the
sons of God, and it doth not
yet appear what we shall be:
but we know that, when he
shall appear, we shall be
like him; for we shall see him
as he is.

1 John 3:2

How would you describe your worldly father and the impact of his love on your life? Now, describe your Heavenly Father and the impact of His love on your life.

_____

_____

_____

_____

_____

_____

_____

_____

_____

_____

_____

_____

_____

_____

_____

_____

_____

_____

_____

# Day 12

Ask, and it shall be given you; seek, and ye shall find; knock, and it shall be opened unto you.

Matthew 7:7

Ask, Seek, Knock. Have you ever applied this promise and nothing in your life changed? If no, tell how your life changed. If yes, tell how you felt and how you petitioned God for answers.

_____

_____

_____

_____

_____

_____

_____

_____

_____

_____

_____

_____

_____

_____

_____

_____

# Day 13

Blessed is the man that walketh not in the counsel of the ungodly, nor standeth in the way of sinners, nor sitteth in the seat of the scornful. But his delight is in the law of the LORD; and in his law doth he meditate day and night. And he shall be like a tree planted by the rivers of water, that bringeth forth his fruit in his season; his leaf also shall not wither; and whatsoever he doeth shall prosper.

Psalm 1:1-3

Define blessed, ungodly, scornful, and delight. Explain what it means for you to delight yourself in the Lord?

_____

_____

_____

_____

_____

_____

_____

_____

_____

_____

_____

_____

_____

_____

_____

_____

# Day 14

Nay, in all these things we are more than conquerors through him that loved us.

Romans 8:37

In this area write the words, "I am more than a conqueror." Meditate on why you are more than a conqueror and list each one as an affirmation. Example: I am more than a conqueror because...

_____

_____

_____

_____

_____

_____

_____

_____

_____

_____

_____

_____

_____

_____

_____

_____

# Day 15

Behold, the LORD'S hand is not shortened, that it cannot save; neither his ear heavy, that it cannot hear.

Isaiah 59:1

What is this scripture saying to your heart?
List three blessed guarantees you get when
you meditate on knowing that the Lord's
hand is not shortened neither His ear heavy.

_____

_____

_____

_____

_____

_____

_____

_____

_____

_____

_____

_____

_____

_____

_____

# Day 16

Many are the afflictions of the righteous: but the Lord delivereth him out of them all.

Psalm 34:19

How does this scripture confirm the word of God for you? Tell of a time that the Lord delivered you from an affliction in your mind and body.

_____

_____

_____

_____

_____

_____

_____

_____

_____

_____

_____

_____

_____

_____

_____

_____

_____

# Day 17

The blessing of the Lord, it
maketh rich, and he addeth
no sorrow with it.

Proverbs 10:22

What does it mean to you to be made rich in the blessings of the Lord? Write a strong declaration for yourself using this scripture.

_____

_____

_____

_____

_____

_____

_____

_____

_____

_____

_____

_____

_____

_____

_____

_____

_____

# Day 18

But my God shall supply all your need according to his riches in glory by Christ Jesus.

Philippians 4:19

Define Need. Do you really know this scripture? If no, state why not. If yes, think of times when this promise became real to you and write about it.

_____

_____

_____

_____

_____

_____

_____

_____

_____

_____

_____

_____

_____

_____

_____

_____

# Day 19

For the LORD God [is] a sun and shield: the LORD will give grace and glory: no good [thing] will he withhold from them that walk uprightly.

Psalms 84:11

What do you think the scripture means when it says, "the Lord will give grace and glory?" Give examples of what it means for you to walk uprightly before the Lord?

_____

_____

_____

_____

_____

_____

_____

_____

_____

_____

_____

_____

_____

_____

_____

_____

_____

# Day 20

I shall not die, but live, and declare the works of the LORD.

Psalm 118:17

# Describe how this promise of God empowers you.

_____

_____

_____

_____

_____

_____

_____

_____

_____

_____

_____

_____

_____

_____

_____

_____

# Day 21

Thou wilt keep him in perfect peace, whose mind is stayed on thee: because he trusteth in thee.

Isaiah 26:3

List a few things that you do to keep your mind stayed on God. Explain how each of these things deepens your relationship of trust in God?

_____

_____

_____

_____

_____

_____

_____

_____

_____

_____

_____

_____

_____

_____

_____

_____

Irene E. Watson is a native of Atlanta, Georgia. Her mother and six siblings are all located in and around metro Atlanta. She has three children, one son-in-law, and three granddaughters. She is dually retired from the United States Army and the Georgia Board of Education. As a retired U.S. Army Human Resources Management and Battalion Executive Officer, she was a major contributor in coordinating and officiating military briefings, training workshops, and medical logistics events.

As a retired Educator, her responsibilities included business education teacher, student liaison, and work-based learning coordinator. She collaborated with colleagues, business owners, and community leaders to develop plans for career education, vocational curricula, and career exploration for high school students.

She is a born again believer who loves serving people, seeing souls saved, and witnessing for the Kingdom of God. She has been graced to organize and spearhead ARISE Women Fellowship. An atmosphere where women of all ages, ethnicities, occupations and education can join together in a safe place to share the love of Jesus Christ.

She has earned an Associate of Arts in Business Administration, Bachelor of Science in Management, Master of Arts in Education and Instructional Leadership, Associate of Biblical Studies from World Changers International Bible School, and a Doctor of Religious Philosophy in Christian Counseling –Minor in Life Coaching from Restoration Theological Seminary.

www.ingramcontent.com/pod-product-compliance
Lightning Source LLC
Chambersburg PA
CBHW071241090426
42736CB00014B/3169